Wanda Space Spy

Written by Zoë Clarke

Illustrated by Luna Valentine

RECORD

Wanda Sky, Space Spy here. My official online channel is now OPEN and I'm ready to tell you all about my job.

I live on Space Station 4, on the outer edge of the galaxy. My official job title is Star Watcher, but 'spy' sounds much cooler. This is my first mission!

There are lots of official watchers here, and we're each in charge of looking at different things. This is the comet crew. They watch for comets and warn Earth when a big one's coming.

This is the satellite crew. They watch all the artificial, or human-made, satellites to make sure they're in the correct position.

This one is now pointing in the right direction!

I look after the animals. Not animals inside the space station, like my friend Wayne here, but groups of stars named after animals.

Wayne

A group of stars is called a constellation.

Bear

Fox

This constellation is called the Bear. And this one is the Fox.

7

In today's star watch session, I want to check the position of a constellation called the Big Dog. First, I check the star chart.

Then, I position the special spy camera to look at it.
Did I mention that one of Big Dog's stars is the brightest in the sky?

My favourite star animal is the swan. I'll reposition the spy camera and we can take a look at it.

I've zoomed to the swan constellation and I can see that some of the stars have wandered off. I can reposition them, but a few of them are still missing.

Something really strange is going on. I'm trying to find the missing swan stars, but I'm being pulled backwards …

I'm spinning around in circles! It's a black hole!

This is my first emergency mission and I'm trying to free myself from being pulled inside a black hole!

I am now speaking to you LIVE from the rim of the black hole! It's very dark inside there, but I can see a swan star!

I've managed to grab the swan star. Next, I'm going to need some technical help from the other watchers back at the space station.

When you need backup from the team, you get it!

The satellite and comet crews have arrived.
Their plan is to use three of the satellites to
bounce a nearby comet into the black hole.

Here comes the comet …
We can watch it shoot forwards and bounce off all three satellites into the black hole. Great work from the space station team!

The comet has burned through the black hole and zoomed off.
I'm now in position to catch the rest of the missing swan stars as they fall through the gap the comet made.

I've put the missing swan stars back in the constellation where they belong. The satellite crew have positioned a special spy camera next to the black hole so we can keep an eye on it.

The swan constellation is complete again. Our mission was a success!

That's all from Space Station 4. This is Wanda Sky, Space Spy, signing off.

Phonics Practice

Say the sound and read the words.

/o/	(w)a

watch   wand   swan   want   washing
wasps   wander

/sh/	-ssi

mission   permission   admission
session   passion

/sh/	-ci

special   official   artificial   optician
musician   magician

Can you say your own sentences using some of the words on these pages?

What other words do you know that are spelled in these ways?

/sh/	-ti

station   position   mention   direction
correction   motion

Common exception words

oh   their   people   Mr   Mrs   looked

We may say some words differently because of our accent.

Talk about the story

Answer the questions:

1 What was Wanda's official job title?

2 What word on page 5 means the same as 'human-made'?

3 Why did Wanda need to go out in the space station rocket?

4 How did sending a comet into the black hole help Wanda?

5 What job would you like to do on Space Station 4?

6 Do you enjoy looking at the night sky? What can you see?

Can you retell the story in your own words?